# Newcas
# Gateshead
# Quayside Guide

Maria Hoy
and
Vanessa Histon

La Tasca   La Tasca

Milk Market

Wesley Square

Sandgate Steps

Central Quayside

Tyne Bridge Publishing
Newcastle Libraries & Information Service

## Acknowledgements

Tyne Bridge Publishing would like to thank Gateshead Council, Mott MacDonald, Newcastle Gateshead Initiative, and Newcastle Tourist Information Centre for their assistance and generosity.

Photographs: courtesy of Gateshead Council, photographer Doug Hall of Bonney's News Agency; courtesy of Newcastle Gateshead Initiative, photographers Graeme Peacock and Alan Bennington; Newcastle Libraries and Information Service; Anna Flowers; Anthony Flowers. Virtual reality image of Music Centre Gateshead courtesy of Foster and Partners; virtual reality image of BALTIC, the Centre for Contemporary Art created by Bridge Ltd. Map: NDS.

ISBN: 1857951417

City of Newcastle upon Tyne Education & Libraries Directorate Newcastle Libraries & Information Service
Tyne Bridge Publishing, 2002

Printed by Elanders Hindson

*Detail from Thomas Oliver's map of Newcastle, 1830.*

## The Quayside

Newcastle Quayside and Gateshead Quays blend the old and the new – medieval and industrial history combine with new art and contemporary architecture to make an exciting area to explore. This booklet provides a guide to the very best sights on both sides of the Tyne with a walk stretching from Sandhill to the Ouseburn. Optional detours into the Close, and across the Gateshead Millennium Bridge returning to Newcastle via the Swing Bridge, are included.

## A little bit of history

Around 122AD, the Romans constructed a bridge, Pons Aelius, near the site of the present Swing Bridge. In 1080 Robert Curthose, son of William the Conqueror, replaced the old Roman fort, constructed to protect the

*Left: The Quayside around 1920.*

bridge, with a wooden castle. Newcastle takes its name from this 'new castle'. The castle was rebuilt in stone in 1168.

The wealth of the city grew around trade – primarily the coal trade – on the Quayside. By the end of the 17th century 90 per cent of ships leaving Newcastle were carrying coal to British and foreign ports. On the return journeys the ships carried ballast including chalk and flint. This ready supply of raw material was the trigger for the growth of industries such as pottery.

The Tyne was once the busiest river in Britain after the Thames and until 1901 it was the premier coal port in the United Kingdom. The Quayside was packed with shops, offices, warehouses and taverns but the town centre gradually moved north, until by the 20th century the Quayside was in decline. The port closed to commercial shipping in 1981 when the work was transferred to areas closer to the river mouth.

*The Quayside around 1745.*

## The rebirth of the riverside

By the mid 1980s much of the riverside was derelict or run down. Tyne and Wear Development Corporation was formed to bring back life and prosperity.

Today Newcastle's Quayside is a thriving mix of offices, hotels, bars, restaurants, clubs and housing, enhanced by landscaping and art work. Gateshead Quays are set to become a focus for art and music. There are still echoes of

the Quayside's past in the names of office developments – Copenhagen, London, Antwerp, Hamburg, Rotterdam, Malmo and Genoa which were all destinations of ships from the Tyne. Several of the thoroughfares are called 'entries' – Johnson, Spencer and Wood named after 19th century owners of property on the Quayside; Wrangham's after a shipbuilder and

*Spicer Lane and Broad Chare are two narrow alleys at the centre of this photograph of around 1895.*

Blue Bell, Porterhouse, Anchor, Flag, and Ravensworth after former pubs. Some thoroughfares keep the mediaeval name 'chare', from the Anglo-Saxon 'cerre' meaning turn.

The Quayside is considered to be one of the best regeneration sites in the country and developments on both sides of the river are helping to inspire dramatic changes in the environment which offer support to the joint bid by Newcastle and Gateshead to be European Capital of Culture in 2008.

# Art on the Riverside

**ART ON THE**
RIVERSIDE
Public Art on the Tyne and the Wear

Art on the Riverside, taking place in North Tyneside, Newcastle, Sunderland and South Tyneside is the largest programme of public art in the UK. Begun in 1995, this programme when complete will consist of a vast range of over 100 artworks and design features created by both local and internationally renowned artists and you can see some of this exciting new art on Newcastle Quayside. In addition, the Weathervane Project has brought together local schools, businesses and artists to create 12 new works (listed at end of book).

*River Siren,*
*Andre Wallace, Sandgate Steps.*

*Blacksmith's Needle, Alan Dawson,*
*Quayside.*

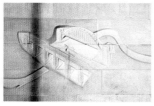

*Relief sculpture, Neil Talbot,*
*Wesley Square.*

*Sandgate*
*Lighthouses,*
*Cate*
*Watkinson,*
*Sandgate Steps*
*& Wesley*
*Square.*

Rudder, Andrew Burton,
Keelman Square.

Column and Steps,
Andrew Burton,
Keelman Square.

Swirle Pavilion,
Raf Fulcher,
Quayside.

Sandgate Steps, ironwork by
Alan Dawson.

River God,
Andre Wallace,
Sandgate.

## A Quayside walk

Agood starting point is at the foot of **THE SIDE**, an ancient street, once the main thoroughfare from the old Tyne Bridge to the centre of Newcastle. Across the road is the **GUILDHALL**, designed by Robert Trollope and opened in 1658. It was a centre for administration and justice, and housed the offices for Newcastle Corporation, the Merchant Adventurers' Court and the Court of Assize. In 1823, Newcastle's celebrated architect, John Dobson, added the colonnaded fish market. The story has it that the fishwives disliked their new place of business so much that they gave Dobson the cold shoulder. Eventually, however, they realised how much more warm and comfortable the new market was compared to their former stalls, dotted about the quay and open to the elements, that they changed their opinion and sent a delegation to Dobson's house to present him with some choice fish for his Christmas dinner. The colonnades were enclosed in 1880 to create a newsroom. A meeting place for the Freemen of Newcastle, it is not open to the public.

West of the Guildhall is another John Dobson design, WATERGATE BUILDINGS, on the line of the medieval Tyne Bridge and its 18th century successor. Remains of the medieval bridge, swept away in devastating floods in 1771, survive in the reputedly haunted cellar of Watergate Buildings. It is now the home of a popular bar, Casa.

Next to Watergate buildings is the SWING BRIDGE, now a listed building and probably the most important surviving hydraulic turning bridge in this country, perhaps anywhere. Opened in 1876, it was designed by William G. later Lord Armstrong, and was then the largest swing bridge in the world. Its unique turning mechanism enabled relatively large ships to navigate to the coal staithes, businesses and factories up river, including Armstrong's own Elswick engineering works. Previously their passage had been blocked by the low 18th century Tyne Bridge, which crossed the river at this point.

*Looking east: the Swing, High Level, Queen Elizabeth II, and King Edward VII Bridges. Redheugh Bridge lies beyond.*

Looking up river, you see the HIGH LEVEL BRIDGE, designed by Robert Stephenson and opened by Queen Victoria in 1849. Her train stopped on the bridge while an address was read to her, but she did not actually get out! Carrying both road and rail traffic, the bridge (a toll bridge until 1937) contributed to the decline of the Quayside as Newcastle's commercial centre, as it brought travellers directly to the higher parts of the town.

Next is the QUEEN ELIZABETH II BRIDGE, which carries the Metro Rapid Transit System across the Tyne. It was opened by Queen Elizabeth II in November 1981.

The KING EDWARD VII BRIDGE has been described as Britain's last great railway bridge. It was opened by King Edward VII in July 1906.

REDHEUGH BRIDGE, designed by Mott, Hay & Anderson (now Mott MacDonald), is the third bridge of

this name. It was opened by Diana, Princess of Wales, in 1983.

*Neptune looks down from the Fish Market.*

Walk east beneath the Swing Bridge. The low red brick building facing the river is a nightclub, Sea, but was the old FISH MARKET, built in 1880. It replaced John Dobson's fish market at the Guildhall. A statue of Neptune, flanked by two fishwives, gazes down from the entrance. The City Coat of Arms forms part of the wrought ironwork gates.

Continuing beneath the massive High Level Bridge, the pub at No. 35 the Close, QUAYSIDE, is probably the oldest

surviving timber framed house in Newcastle. It is typical of a medieval merchant's house, set back from the river with long, narrow warehouses and its own wharf.

You might see fishermen here taking advantage of the now clean conditions in the Tyne which supports salmon and trout. If you like, continue your walk west up river and look towards the Gateshead bank to see **DUNSTON STAITHES**. This scheduled Ancient

*The Copthorne Hotel, built on the line of the old Town Wall*

Monument is one of the largest timber structures in the world. It was opened in 1893 by the North Eastern Railway. Coal would be transported here from the collieries in north Durham and loaded onto ships for transportation to the fires and furnaces of Britain and Europe. At its peak, the staithes handled two million tons of coal a year.

Now you can either turn back down the Quayside to walk down river, or continue into the Close.

*Dunston Staithes, 1920.*

Turn right between the Copthorne Hotel and Bridge Court to enter **THE CLOSE**, one of Newcastle's oldest streets, an area of land reclaimed from the river

*Turnbull's Warehouse towers over the Close. The stone post reads 'Javel Groupe', the name of an ancient alley that ran down to the river here.*

between the 13th and 15th centuries as rubbish tipped into the water became landfill. The name refers to the narrowness or closeness of the street. The Close was a prosperous area of Newcastle, home to wealthy merchants, burgesses and members of the aristocracy until the 18th century. One important building which once stood here was the mayor's sumptuous Mansion House.

To the left is **BREAKNECK STAIRS**, the first of a series of steep stairs leading from the riverside area to the higher part of town. You can see remains of the 13th and 14th century Town Wall by the stairs. Near here stood Close Gate, demolished in 1792, one of the ancient gates in the wall. Beside the wall and stairs is the steep landscaping of **HANOVER GARDENS**, an award-winning design. **TURNBULL'S WAREHOUSE**, above and to the east, like a castle in imposing Gothic red brick, was built as a printing works in 1895. It is now a listed building of Manhattan style apartments.

As the Quayside became more crowded and insanitary during the late 18th and 19th centuries, families who could afford to move away did so. Soon, the once fine buildings in The Close became tenemented dwellings for the poor, and later housed glass, iron and soap works and warehouses.

Some important and well-preserved ancient buildings still stand in The Close. The lively **COOPERAGE** pub, at Nos. 32-34 is a 16th century stone building. According to local tradition, the timber came from a ship which sank

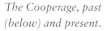

*The Cooperage, past (below) and present.*

in the Tyne. Because of limited availability of level land beside the steep slope, the house was extended upwards rather than outwards. A new storey was added every 100 years or so using Dutch bricks which probably arrived in Newcastle as ships' ballast. The pub takes its name from a cooper (barrel-maker) who had his business here.

Continue down the Close into **SANDHILL**. At low tide, this was, as its name suggests, a hill of sand. First recorded in 1310, Sandhill was the market place for the town and at the heart of maritime trade largely with the Baltic ports. It was also the place for entertainment, proclamations, bonfires, bull baiting, plays and public executions. Some fine houses dating from the 16th century survive. When they were built they had shops or stores at ground level and living quarters above. Castle Stairs lead down from Castle Garth to Sandhill. If you have time, climb the stairs for a fascinating view of the rear of these ancient houses.

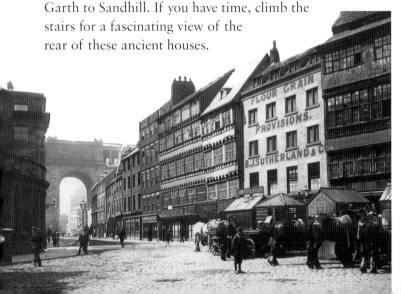

*Bessie Surtees House, with the High Level Bridge beyond.*

No. 41 is **BESSIE SURTEES HOUSE**, originally two houses, one dating from the 16th century, faced with brick early
in the 18th century, with an elegant Georgian frontage,
sash windows and fine plasterwork. The second house was
built in the 1637 and keeps its original facade. It was from
this house in 1772, that Bessie Surtees, daughter of a
wealthy banker, eloped with John Scott, a coal fitter's son.
Fortunately, the marriage was a long and happy one and
John Scott rose to become Lord Eldon, Chancellor of
England. Bessie Surtees House is preserved by English
Heritage, and some rooms are open to the public on week-
days. They have elaborate plaster ceilings, 17th century
panelling and unique fireplaces. The buildings at No. 40,
33 (once town house of the Derwentwater family), and 32
(the Red House), date from around the same period.

*The High Level Bridge, with beyond it the Tyne Bridge and Gateshead Millennium Bridges.*

Returning to the Quayside, you are almost beneath the **TYNE BRIDGE**, which was opened in 1928 by King

George V. It bears a striking resemblance to Sydney Harbour Bridge and is sometimes described as a prototype, but this is not the case. Both bridges were built by Dorman Long and company, and although the Sydney Harbour Bridge was started first, the Tyne Bridge, because of its shorter span, was completed earlier. The huge pillars supporting the Tyne Bridge were intended to contain warehouses, but the interior floors were never completed. They also contained passenger and goods lifts to service the Quayside. Even so, the bridge contributed to the decline of the Quayside, as it brought more travellers directly to the higher area of the town.

*The view from Gateshead the morning after the Great Fire of 6 October 1854.*

If you had been standing on this spot on 6 October 1854, you would have witnessed a terrifying spectacle. Shortly after midnight, a fire was discovered in Wilson's Mill on the Gateshead bank. The blaze quickly spread to surrounding buildings including a chemical warehouse. Huge crowds had gathered on the Quayside to watch the conflagration. At about 3.15 in the morning, there was an enormous explosion, and burning debris was flung across the Tyne, igniting ships on the river and buildings on the Newcastle side. The damage was devastating. Over 50 died,

hundreds were made homeless, and many of Newcastle's medieval streets and buildings were destroyed.

Looking to your left, you will see some of the elegant buildings which replaced the narrow alleys destroyed in the fire. Much of the redevelopment was undertaken by John Dobson, who, ironically, lost his own son in the disaster. Many of the buildings housed shipping offices, and their grandeur testifies to Newcastle's importance as a port. One of the first is **EXCHANGE BUILDINGS**. It was designed in 1861-2 by William Parnell.

Look up **KING STREET** for a wonderful view of **ALL SAINTS CHURCH**, which was designed in the classical style by David Stephenson and consecrated in 1789. According to one story, on the day the church opened, David Burdikin, a soldier in the

Cheshire Militia, stood on his head on top of the tower! His reasons for doing so are not recorded. The church is now a Grade One listed building. It became redundant in 1961 but today it is once again a church – The Anglican Catholic Church of St Willibrord with All Saints.

At 31 the Quayside is **THREE INDIAN KINGS HOUSE**. It was formerly a pub of the same name. In records of 1666 it appears as The Kings; it became

*The Custom House.*

Three Indian Kings House by 1735. The name is thought to refer to the three wise men in the nativity story.

The **CUSTOM HOUSE** stands at No. 39, a survivor of the 1854 fire. It was built in 1766 to replace an earlier Custom House near the Guildhall. The frontage, designed by Sydney Smirke, dates from 1833. Above the door is the Hanoverian Royal Coat of Arms.

Walk past the exceedingly narrow Trinity Chare and turn left into **BROAD CHARE**. Before the fire, the Quayside was covered by a network of narrow, cramped alleys called

*A narrow Broad Chare, around 1890. Below, Broad Chare and Baltic Chambers, the Law Courts to the right.*

chares. After the fire only seven of the 16 original chares remained between Sandhill and Broad Chare. Broad Chare, as the name suggests, was wider than the others, wide enough for a cart to pass through. On the left of the street is **LIVE THEATRE**, housed in a converted warehouse. Some of the North East's finest playwrights, including Alan Plater, Julia Darling and Lee Hall have written for the Live. The script for the film *Billy Elliott* had early readings here. Actors associated with the theatre include Robson Green, Tim Healy and Val McLane.

Further up Broad Chare is **TRINITY HOUSE**, home of the Guild of Masters and Mariners who acquired the site in 1505. They administered river traffic, collected dues, provided lighthouses and buoys and trained river pilots. Go through the iron gateway into the courtyard. The banqueting hall is on your left, the rigging loft on your right, and the almshouses straight ahead. Broad Chare is said to be haunted by the ghost of Martha Wilson, a

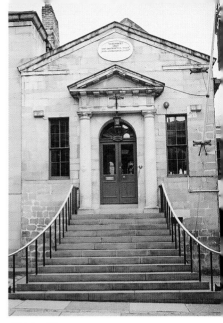

*Trinity House.*

seaman's widow who hanged herself in her room in the almshouses in 1817. If you are in Broad Chare at night, you may hear the rustle of a woman's dress, accompanied by a soft chuckle.

Back in Broad Chare, a left turn leads past the chapel window which dates from 1794. At the top of the Chare is Dog Bank, a steep footpath leading to All Saints Church. To continue your walk, retrace your steps to the foot of Broad Chare.

On your left are the **LAW COURTS**, opened in 1990. The

*Searching for a bargain at Paddy's market on Sandgate around 1900.*

red sandstone was chosen to blend in with the nearby red brick warehouses, and the round windows have a nautical theme.

A little further on was the **MILK MARKET**. There had been a milk market at the Quayside from at least 1717. Until 1827, agricultural workers gathered there, waiting to be hired by local farmers. Although food was sold there, the market was far from sanitary. It was the site of the Sandgate Midden, where street sweepings and waste from slaughter houses and other establishments was tipped. The contents of the midden were sold for manure, and taken away by keel or farmer's cart.

On Saturdays the Milk Market was home to Paddy's Market where old clothes were sold. Originally the clothes for sale were laid on straw in the street and displayed on the remains of the old town walls. Paddy's Market continued into the second half of the 20th century. One long-standing Quayside market which still continues

*The Sunday Market extends right along the Quayside today.*

today is the Sunday Market. In 1880, you could buy a full range of goods, including ice cream, and be entertained by escapologists and orators.

Cross the road at the traffic lights. This area is **SANDGATE**, named after the gate in the Town Wall which stood on the sand here. Sandgate was once narrow, densely populated, filthy and squalid. The slums were cleared during the 19th century as the Quayside was widened and extended eastward.

The pink granite obelisk in WESLEY SQUARE, is the WESLEY MEMORIAL, a drinking fountain originally erected in nearby Milk Market. It commemorates the first sermon preached in Newcastle by the father of methodism, John Wesley, in May 1742. The sandstone wall follows the line of the old Town Wall which had extended along the Quayside and was demolished in 1763. The carvings are by Neil Talbot and represent places on the Tyne: Hadrian's Wall, Bardon Mill, Haydon Bridge, Hexham Abbey, Corbridge, Cherryburn (birthplace of celebrated engraver Thomas Bewick), Prudhoe Castle, George Stephenson's birthplace, Lemington glass cone, Dunston Staithes, Tyne Bridge, shipyards, St Paul's Church at Jarrow, Arbeia Roman Fort at South Shields, Tynemouth Priory – and a trawler named *Talbot*. Alan Dawson's ironwork railings echo the maritime theme.

The LIGHTHOUSE is one of three illuminated features (the others are at Sandgate Steps) by Cate Watkinson. Each lighthouse has 36 hand made stained glass panels.

Further on and leading up from the left are SANDGATE STEPS. The two bronze sculptures are by Andre Wallace. River God, at the bottom of the steps is 35 feet high. His mouth is open, because the original concept included him breathing fire from a gas jet. At the top of the steps is the

20 foot high River Siren. There are also carvings by Neil Talbot, taken from engravings in T.H. Hair's *A Series of Views of the Collieries in the Counties of Northumberland and Durham* (1841). Graciela Ainsworth has engraved words from the famous Geordie song, *The Keel Row* into the steps. The ironwork railings, handrails and lamp columns are designed by Alan Dawson.

From the top of the steps you can see the clock tower of the **KEELMEN'S HOSPITAL**. Because larger ships could not navigate the upper stretches of the Tyne at Newcastle, coal had to be brought down river in flat-bottomed boats

*Sandgate Steps.*

called keels, and loaded onto ocean-going vessels. Keelmen, who operated the keels did a difficult, strenuous and dangerous job, and their sense of brotherhood was strong. They contributed to the care of their sick and injured

colleagues and the widows and orphans of fellow keelmen in 1701, by funding the building of the hospital.

The **MALMAISON HOTEL** (left, and above before its transformation) takes its name from the home of Josephine, wife of Napoleon Bonaparte. It is housed in the former Co-operative Wholesale Society warehouse, built between 1897 and 1900. The Co-op was always progressive and decided to build the warehouse from the very latest material – concrete reinforced with iron. This building is probably the oldest surviving large-scale ferro-concrete building in the country.

In **KEELMAN SQUARE**, next door, are two bronze sculptures, Column and Steps and Rudder, both by Andrew Burton.

The architecture of **THE PITCHER AND PIANO** comple-
ments the maritime theme of the Quayside. The sandstone
wall represents the hull of a ship and the glass front echoes
the scaffolding of the Tyne's great shipyards.

Continue east along the river, passing the Gateshead
Millennium Bridge, to the **SWIRLE PAVILION** (right),
topped by a golden globe in a metal sphere, designed by
Raf Fulcher. Inside the pavilion are the names of former

Quayside wharves and
destinations of the ships
leaving the Tyne. The
name Swirle comes from
the Swirle or Squirrel
burn which ran into the
river near this point.

*The Swirle, 1926. The Half
Moon pub is on the left.*

*Half Moon Square and St Ann's Wharf.*

The **ST ANN'S WHARF** building, up the steps, behind the Swirle Pavilion, surrounds a courtyard called **HALF MOON SQUARE**, after a former pub in the Swirle.

There is a stone half moon in a plinth in the middle of the courtyard. One of the residents of St Ann's Wharf is engineering consultants Mott MacDonald, who, as Mott, Hay, and Anderson, designed the Tyne Bridge and Redheugh Bridge. Their latest project is the Music Centre, Gateshead.

**THE BLACKSMITH'S NEEDLE**, 7.6 metres tall, was created by the British Artist Blacksmiths' Association, to a design by Alan Dawson. It was unveiled by percussionist Evelyn Glennie in 1997. The tiers represent, from the base, sight, touch, sound, taste, smell, and the sixth sense. Some tiers also include items reflecting a maritime theme. Can you spot a mermaid, a seahorse and a swordfish? A bell hangs from the centre of the needle.

You are now in the area which used to be called North Shore, which, before the Quayside was extended in the

*Mariner's Wharf. The Sailors' Bethel and the Ouseburn can be seen in the distance.*

mid-19th century, was home to several early shipyards, wharves, a ropery, ships' chandlers, mast makers and other river trades. This is the site of Dandy Gears, a wooden jetty with three spouts, so three ships could be loaded with coal at once. Between 1870 and 1969, a railway connected the Quayside warehouses, wharves and manufacturers through a tunnel to Manors Station.

Further east, and above, on City Road is ST ANN'S CHURCH, built in 1768 using stones from a demolished section of the Town Wall.

In the distance, on the left, jutting above the Glasshouse Bridge, you can see part of the BYKER WALL, a world famous housing project. To the right of this is a building with an impressive pagoda-style roof. It is OUSEBURN BUILDING, designed in 1893 as a school, but now a business centre.

The Victoria Tunnel emerged west of the Ouseburn. Over two miles long, the tunnel carried coal on a railway under the city from Spital Tongues Colliery to the river.

The grey spire behind the flats belongs to the **SAILORS' BETHEL**, opened in 1877 as a non-conformist church with a resident missionary. During its lifetime it has served as a community centre, Danish seamen's church, and a doll factory. An oil painting of the building, made by L.S. Lowry in 1965, is in the Laing Art Gallery.

*The pointed spire of the Sailors' Bethel.*

At the end of the flats on **MARINER'S WHARF** is *Confluence*, a metal sculpture, part of the Weathervane Project (see list at the end of the book).

At the end of the walkway is the **OUSEBURN WATER SPORTS ASSOCIATION**, opened in 1994. The wave-like roof shape continues the maritime theme. During the industrial revolution, Ouseburn was a major glass making centre. Forty per cent of the country's glass was once made here. There were also several potteries in the area, including the world-famous Maling works.

Retrace your steps west along the river. Looking to your right, up the hill, you can see the back of a statue. It is actually a drinking fountain, with two troughs, one for animals and one for humans. It was erected in honour of Colonel William L. Blenkinsopp Coulson, who campaigned on behalf of mistreated animals and humans. As you look to the west you will see spectacular views of the Tyne bridges, including the graceful sweep of the newest bridge.

Now cross **GATESHEAD MILLENNIUM BRIDGE**, the
most recent of the Tyne's historic bridges. Opened to the
public on 17 September, 2001, and officially opened by the
Queen in May 2002, the bridge was constructed in
Wallsend then brought up river and manoeuvred into
position by one of the world's largest floating cranes. This
bridge is unique – the world's first tilting bridge. The
whole structure pivots upwards like a closed eye slowly
opening, so that ships can pass under the arch. Each
opening and closing takes around four minutes. It is
expected to open at least 200 times a year, but is so energy
efficient that each opening costs just £3.60. A spectacular
computer-controlled lighting system makes the bridge
equally stunning at night.

*The future – a computer projection of the completed BALTIC, the Centre for Contemporary Art.*

To the left of the bridge is **BALTIC, the CENTRE FOR CONTEMPORARY ART**. The building was opened as a flour mill by Rank in 1949. Like all the Rank mills, it was named after a sea. It closed in 1983, but is now being reborn as one of the biggest art spaces in Europe. With five galleries, totalling over 3000 square metres, **BALTIC** also houses artists' studios, a cinema/lecture space, a library and archive for the study of contemporary art, a shop and restaurants, including one on the rooftop with stunning views of Tyneside. Even while the gallery was under construction, the space was used for installations by internationally famous artists such as Anish Kapoor. The Centre will house a constantly changing programme rather than a permanent collection. It is due to open in 2002.

Having enjoyed the view up and down river from the vantage point of the bridge, step off the bridge into Baltic Square, a new contemporary arts square linking the south bank developments. The Square was first used as part of the 'Music for a New Crossing' event which celebrated the opening of the Gateshead Millennium Bridge. A new cultural quarter including luxury hotels, bars, restaurants and clubs is being developed on the Gateshead Quays.

Walk up the steps ahead of you and turn right. The building behind the wall on the riverside is HMS *Calliope*, the Royal Naval Reserve Training Centre which opened in 1968.

Opposite, on top of the bank, the MUSIC CENTRE GATESHEAD is under construction. This will provide world class music facilities, including concert halls, a music school and a music library, as well as a permanent home for the Northern Sinfonia and Folkworks (which promotes traditional music). Designed by Foster and Partners it will boast a 1,650 seat concert hall, a 400 seat hall, plus rehearsal and educational areas and resource centres. Everything from Bach to barber-shop will be catered for including classical, rock, pop, jazz, folk, brass, choral,

*The future – how the Music Centre Gateshead will look when it is complete.*

world music and of course schools' music. The centre will be really seven buildings in one, designed from the inside-out and clothed by a spectacular curved roof.

Continue towards the Swing Bridge past the Tuxedo Princess, a floating nightclub. There is a plaque on the pillar of the Tyne Bridge commemorating the site of Wilson's Spinning Mill where the 1854 fire began.

On the hill to your left is **ST MARY'S CHURCH**, built in the 12th century, and the first church in Gateshead. It is

*The past – Gateshead, St Mary's Church and Bottle Bank, and the Swing Bridge, 1924.*

now the **GATESHEAD QUAYS VISITOR CENTRE**. The centre describes not only the exciting new developments in the area, but also the history of Gateshead Quays. In 1080 the church on this site was the scene of a violent clash between native Saxons and the Norman forces of occupation.

Not visible from the Quayside, but behind the Music Centre, are the arches of Oakwellgate, a railway viaduct which used to carry Brandling Junction Railway over Gateshead. Oakwellgate Station stood on the viaduct, 20 feet above street level. It closed to passenger traffic in 1844.

*Pipewellgate, with the High Level Bridge to the right, around 1879.*

Across the road from the church the Tyne Bridge Hilton International is under construction in BOTTLE BANK. This was the first area of Gateshead to be settled and Roman coins were found during excavations here. The name has nothing to do with bottles. It comes from the Saxon word 'botl' meaning a house or dwelling.

The land which can be seen on the opposite side of the Swing Bridge is PIPEWELLGATE. Bronze age swords, spearheads and daggers were found near here when the Tyne was dredged between 1867 and 1882. There was once a well here, with water probably running through a wooden pipe. Looking at the steep, landscaped river bank, it is difficult to imagine that this was once one of the busiest and most crowded areas of Gateshead. Ropes, glass, bricks, clay pipes, paper, pottery, textiles and chemicals were all made in this area. Crammed beside the workshops, were shops, taverns and houses. Pipewellgate, at its narrowest, was only seven and a half feet wide and health visitors described it as a vile place. It escaped the great fire of 1854, but during the second half of the 19th century anyone who could afford to do so moved away. The area continued to decline, and by the 1930s slum clearance orders led to the rehousing of the remaining population.

*Rolling Moon by Colin Rose.*

Further along the Gateshead bank is the RIVERSIDE SCULPTURE PARK with works by artists such as Andy Goldsworthy and Hideo Furuta.

The building on the corner of the Swing Bridge, now a restaurant, was originally the River Police Station – see the photograph of Gateshead in 1924. If you choose to cross the road for a closer look take great care as the traffic is fast and there is a blind bend in the road to your left.

Turning on to the Swing Bridge head back towards Newcastle and look at the skyline ahead, where the view of the steep riverbank is stunning. The Moot Hall can be seen above the Waterside Hotel with the castle keep to the left.

# THE WEATHERVANE PROJECT

**Weathervane**

The Weathervane Project brought together local schools, businesses and artists to create 12 pieces of art on the riverside:

*Copthorne Hotel* Aluminium and glass wind sculpture depicting the Quayside fire, designed by Chillingham Road Primary School with Cate Watkinson and Jane Dudman.

*All Saints Church* Stained glass window panels by Kingston Park Primary School with Sue Woolhouse and Jim Roberts.

*Eldon Chambers* Exterior sign by Wingrove Road Primary School with Helen Law and Effie Burns.

*Live Theatre* Sandblasted window by Parkway Special School with Malcolm Smith and Lucy Broadhead.

*Sandgate House* 'To Catch a Fish' by St Mary's School with Northern Freeform.

*Malmaison Hotel* 'Aspirations' sculpture by Kenton School with Sue Woolhouse and Jim Roberts.

*Quayside House* Glass wall panels by Ashfield Nursery School with Sue Woolhouse, Cate Watkinson, Lucy Broadhead and Effie Burns.

*Ouseburn Water Sports Association* Sundial sculpture by Atkinson road Nursery School with Helen Law and Jane Gower.

*St Ann's Wharf* 'Neptune's Chair' sculpture by Walker Comprehensive School with Helen Law and Effie Burns.

*Sailors' Bethel* Glass canopy by Byker Primary School with Cate Watkinson and Jane Dudman.

*Mariner's Wharf* 'Confluence' sculpture by Christchurch Primary School with Sue Woolhouse and Jim Roberts.

Further reading on the Quayside published by Tyne Bridge Publishing at Newcastle Libraries & Information Service:

*Crossing the Tyne* by Frank Manders and Richard Potts.

*On the Waterfront: A Historical Tour of Newcastle's Quayside*, by Ian Ayris and Patricia Sheldon.

*Bygone West Quayside and the Close* by Jack and John Leslie.

*Bygone Quayside and the Chares* by Jack and John Leslie.

These books are on sale at bookshops, Tourist Information Centres and Libraries.

Check out the Tyne Bridge Publishing website on:

www.newcastle.gov.uk/tynebridgepublishing

*Children at the Milk Market fountain in 1894.*

| | |
|---|---|
| ➡ ONE WAY STREETS | 🅿 PARKING |
| ◣ GREEN SPACES | ✝ CHURCH |
| [WC] TOILET | ⬠ THEATRE |
| [♿WC] DISABLED TOILET | 𝕸 MUSEUM/GALLERY |

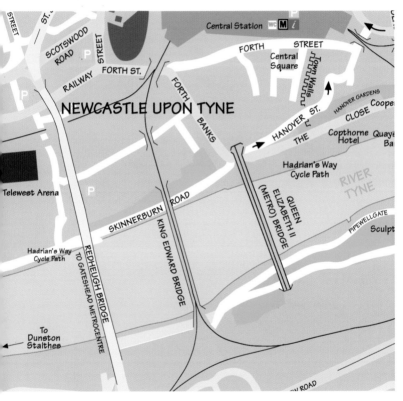

# NEWCASTLE UPON TYNE

Central Station [WC] [M] [i]

SCOTSWOOD ROAD
ST. STREET
RAILWAY
FORTH ST.
FORTH BANKS
FORTH STREET
Central Square
Forth St.
Town Walls
Hanover St.
HANOVER GARDENS
CLOSE
Cooper
Copthorne Hotel
Quaye
Ba
THE
Hadrian's Way Cycle Path
RIVER TYNE
Telewest Arena
🅿
SKINNERBURN ROAD
KING EDWARD BRIDGE
QUEEN ELIZABETH II (METRO) BRIDGE
PIPEWELLGATE
Sculpt
Hadrian's Way Cycle Path
REDHEUGH BRIDGE
TO GATESHEAD METROCENTRE
To Dunston Stalthes

0       500 METRES (APPROX)
0       440 YARDS (APPROX)